Zoobooks®

Parrots

www.zoobooks.com

Parrots are very popular with people, for several obvious reasons. To begin with, they are beautiful. Many parrot species are covered from head to tail with brilliantly colored feathers. And many of them have other ornaments, such as crests, that add to their beauty. There are only a few other groups of birds in the world that can match the splendor of the parrots.

People are also impressed and charmed by the ability that some parrots have to "talk." In some cases, this ability seems truly astounding. The African gray parrot, for example, can be taught to mimic men, women, children, and other animals. There have been parrots that could recite speeches or tell a whole string of jokes. At times, parrots can be so good at saying words and phrases that we are almost convinced that they know what they are saying.

But, of course, they don't really understand any of it. They are just good "copycats," with an excellent knack for imitating the sounds they hear. There is a mystery to this, all the same. It seems that wild parrots in the jungle don't imitate the sounds of other birds and animals. Among captive parrots, the African gray parrot is the best "talker."

The "talking" of parrots appeals to us because it seems so similar to our own behavior. And parrots do other things that are appealing for the same reason. For instance, they are usually very loyal to their mates. Many times, the "husband" and "wife" in a mated pair of parrots stay together for life. They are good parents, too. While most bird parents push their young out of the nest as soon as possible, parrots may allow their young to stay around (and be fed) for a long time.

With most parrot species, it is easy to tell the males and the females apart. Males usually have more colorful feathers, which they use to attract the females. However, in some parts of the world, female parrots and parakeets may be as brightly colored as the males—and this makes it almost impossible to tell them apart.

Some types of parrots can live a long time. Cockatoos in zoos have lived more than 70 years— and some people claim these parrots can live even longer than that.

A flock of parrots in flight is one of nature's most beautiful sights. These are galah (guh-lah) cockatoos from Australia.

The **wonderful variety of parrots** adds a rainbow of colors to the animal world. A few parrots have feathers that are dull brown or tan. But most of them are dressed in vivid reds, greens, yellows, and blues. There are more than 300 different species, and some of the most beautiful are shown here.

GOLDEN CONURE
Aratinga guarouba

YELLOW–HEADED AMAZON
Amazona oratrix

SCARLET MACAW
Ara macao

BUDGERIGAR
Melopsittacus undulatus

GREAT BLACK (PALM) COCKATOO
Probosciger aterrimus goliath

AFRICAN GRAY PARROT
Psittacus erithacus

LILAC–CROWNED AMAZON
Amazona finschi

BLOSSOM–HEADED PARAKEET
Psittacula roseata

MASCARENE PARROT
Mascarinus mascarinus
(Extinct)

EASTERN ROSELLA
Platycercus eximius

SULPHUR–CRESTED COCKATOO
Cacatua galerita

COCKATIEL
Nymphicus hollandicus

2

GALAH
Eolophus roseicapillus

HAWK-HEADED PARROT
Deroptyus accipitrinus

ST. VINCENT'S AMAZON
Amazona guildingii

-BILLED PARROTS
anygnathus egalorynchos

ULTRAMARINE LORY
Vini ultramarina

KEA
Nestor notabilis

WHITE-NAPED LORY
Lorius albidinuchus

NTH MACAW
dorhynchus icinthinus

BUFFON'S MACAW
Ara ambigua

BLUE-CROWNED RACKET-
TAILED PARROT
Prioniturus discurus platenae

PESQUET'S PARROT
Psittrichas fulgidus

PAINTED CONURE
Pyrrhura picta

BUFF-FACED PYGMY PARROT
Micropsitta pusio

KAKAPO
Strigops hapbroptilus

BLUE-AND-GOLD MACAW
-*Ara ararauna*

MASKED LOVEBIRD
Agapornis personata

3

A **parrot's body** is made for living in a tropical forest. In such a place, there are many brightly colored leaves, flowers, and fruits. The bright colors of the parrot blend in and help the birds hide from predators. When a parrot perches on a branch high up in a tree, it may look like a piece of fruit or a flower to a predator. Parrots get most of their food from trees by gathering seeds, nuts, and fruits. On these pages you will see how their bodies are specially designed for feeding and foraging in the forest.

For a bird, a parrot has a rather plump body. It must have strong muscles in its legs and wings in order to fly, or even to climb around in the trees.

The feathers of parrots are like flags. Every parrot species in the world has its own special colors, just as every country in the world has its own flag. Each parrot can tell if another parrot is a member of the same species by looking at the colors it is wearing.

Parrot feet have an unusually strong grip. Each foot has four long toes. Two of the toes point forward and two point backward. This arrangement makes it easy for parrots to grab slippery seeds, nuts, or fruits. They can grab a branch so tightly they can hang upside down if they want to. They can even stand on one foot while they eat with the other!

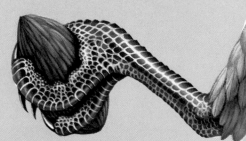

Unlike any other bird, a parrot can use its foot to bring food up to its mouth. It can wrap its toes around a piece of food in the same way that you can wrap your fingers around a glass.

...ke all flying birds, parrots ...ve many bones that are ...llow. This helps to make ...eir bodies lighter, so it is ...sier for them to fly. But even ...th hollow bones parrots are ...avier than most birds. They ...ve to flap their wings very ...t to stay up in the air.

All parrots have hooked bills, and this is really the easiest way to see if a bird is a parrot. But there is a great deal of variety in the shapes of the hooks. This is because different kinds of parrots need different types of hooks for eating different kinds of foods.

SLENDER-BILLED CORELLA

RED-CAPPED PARROT

A few parrots dig up roots and bulbs from the ground. For these birds, the upper part of the bill is long, so they can use their bills like shovels.

Some parrots use their bills to scrape seeds out of pods. For this reason, their bills are pointed and very sharp, like paring knives.

PALM COCKATOO

This bird likes to eat nuts that have hard shells. It has a big, thick bill that can crush even the toughest nut.

LORY

Lories don't dig, scrape, or crack anything. They get most of their food by drinking nectar and eating pollen from flowers. Lories don't need heavy-duty beaks, so their bills are small and weak.

Different kinds of parrots have so many different kinds of names that it may seem confusing. But all parrots belong to only three main groups: (1) the *parrots and parakeets,* (2) the *lories and lorikeets,* and (3) the *cockatoos.*

The parrot and parakeet group is the largest. It includes the biggest parrots, called *macaws,* and the smallest, called *pygmy parrots.* Among the other members of the group are the *conures* (**kahn**-yurz), *keas* (**kee**-yuhz), and *Amazons.*

On these pages, you will see some of the major types of parrots—and learn how you can tell one from another.

GREEN-WINGED MACAW

Many kinds of parrots have a small ring of bare skin around each eye, like the Amazon at left. But only macaws have large patches of skin on the sides of their faces.

IMPERIAL AMAZON

PURPLE-BELLIED LORY

Lories have remarkable tongues for collecting nectar and pollen from flowers. The tongue looks like a tiny brush with hundreds of little bristles. The lory can poke its tongue into a flower and brush up the nectar and pollen.

1

3

The tails of parrots come in many shapes and sizes. They may be short and square, like an Amazon parrot's tail ①, or long and pointed, like a parakeet's ②. The tails of racket-tailed parrots are really strange. There are two feathers in the middle that look like long tennis rackets ③, but the rest of the tail is short and square.

The red areas on this map show where parrots live. As you can see, most of them live in warm parts of the world. But a few are found in places where you'd never expect to find them.

SLATY-HEADED PARAKEET

Slaty-headed parakeets live farther north than any other parrot species. They are found in the mountains of Afghanistan ①.

1

The kea of New Zealand ③ likes the cold so much that it rolls around in the snow.

The tip of South America has some of the worst weather in the world. Austral conures live there ②.

KEA

2

AUSTRAL CONURE

3

OLDEN-MANTLED RACKET-TAILED PARROT

LONG-TAILED PARAKEET

Most cockatoos carry crests of pointed feathers on the tops of their heads. A cockatoo can raise or lower its crest whenever it wants.

RED-BREASTED PYGMY PARROT

2

Pygmy parrots have sharp spines on the tips of their tails. The spines dig into the bark of a tree and hold the parrot steady while it looks for insects to eat.

MAJOR MITCHELL'S COCKATOO

7

Like many parrots, these Blue-and-yellow Macaws spend a lot of their time fighting with each other.

Families are important in the lives of parrots. Father and mother parrots work as a team to hatch their eggs and care for their young.

As you can see at right, the family nest is usually very simple. Most parrots just find a big hole in a tree. Most of the time, the eggs are simply laid on the dust and deadwood already in the hole. However, there are some parrots that nest in different ways, as you will see below.

ADELAIDE ROSELLAS

ORANGE-FRONTED PARAKEETS

In dry places, where there aren't many trees, parrots may build their nests in cactus plants.

A few species build nests on the ground. They sometimes use holes or cracks in rocks to shelter the nests.

KEA

When baby parrots hatch from their eggs, they only have a thin covering of down on their backs. Their eyes don't open until they are nearly two weeks old. They are almost helpless for the first month of their lives. After the chicks hatch, the mother stays with them, while the father goes out to get food.

MONK PARAKEETS

There are even parrots that dig nest holes in termite mounds. The termites don't seem to bother the parrots.

Most parrot nests are only large enough for a single family. But monk parakeets build huge nests of grass that can be big enough for many families. The nests are like apartment houses, with separate "rooms" for each family.

This tiny chick is about three weeks old. Its first real feathers are just beginning to grow. At this stage, the feathers look like pins, so they are called *pinfeathers*.

Parrot eggs look a lot like chicken eggs. They are round and almost pure white. After the eggs are laid, the mother and father take turns sitting on them—although the mother usually does more sitting than the father. It takes about three weeks for the eggs of most parrots to hatch.

Only a few types of parrots gather twigs and leaves to line their nests. Hanging parrots have a strange way of carrying these things back to the nest. They stuff everything into their tail feathers, so the nesting material won't get in the way when they fly. This makes the parrots look like flying pincushions!

MACAWS

Most kinds of parrots are very sociable. They like to gather in large flocks. There may be more than a thousand parrots in a single flock.

Male and female parrots almost always live together in pairs. Some parrots, like the lovebirds at right, show an almost human affection for each other. They like to sit together, rubbing their bills together and preening each other's feathers.

FISCHER'S LOVEBIRDS

11

Do you think it would be fun to have a wild parrot for a pet? Or some other wild animal? Do you imagine your friends being jealous? When you daydream about having a wild pet you might have some of the same thoughts that appear on these pages.

How about a living teddy bear for a pet? It might be fun to stroke its fur and feed it honey.

Why wait for the circus to come to town? Your own elephant will give you a ride whenever you like—and maybe help you wash the car!

Why settle for a goldfish or a hamster, when you could have a pair of beautiful fig parrots instead?

Have you ever seen anything that looks as cute and cuddly as a bushbaby?

If you have an extra swimming pool, a friendly alligator is just the thing for you. One thing is certain—you'll be the only person on your block that has one.

Your friends will really think you're rich if you own a macaw. Some of these beautiful birds cost more than $5,000.

You'll always have something to talk to when you've got a pair of cockatoos.

Wild parrots belong in the wild. So do all other wild animals. It might be fun to think about, but actually *owning* a wild animal would be very difficult. And no matter how hard you might try, you could never make it as happy as it would be in the wild.

A full-grown bear with great-big claws can be hard on your furniture.

Unless you're a millionaire, you could go broke trying to buy enough food for an elephant.

Wild animals can make an awful mess. These parrots like to spread seeds and other foods all over the place.

Bushbabies are night animals. When you want to sleep, they want to play.

You never know when an alligator might suddenly get hungry.

Cockatoos like to start shrieking very early in the morning. They'll get you up every day at the crack of dawn.

Macaws like to crack things open with their big, strong beaks.

Wild parrots are in danger today. People capture too many of them to sell as pets. Also, the forests they live in are being chopped down so people can build farms or sell the wood.

If the destruction of the forests and the trapping of birds are not stopped, there will soon be no more beautiful wild parrots. There is one thing we can all do to help. We can refuse to buy parrots that have been taken from the wild. We can also ask our friends to do the same.

RAINBOW LORIES

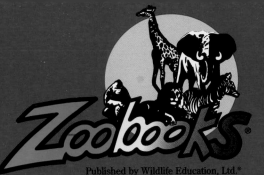

Zoobooks®

Published by Wildlife Education, Ltd.®

ON THE COVER:
A Scarlet Macaw

Created and Written by
John Bonnett Wexo

Scientific Consultants
James Dolan, Ph.D.
Director, Animal Collections
San Diego Zoo &
San Diego Wild Animal Park

The Late Kenton C. Lint
Curator of Birds Emeritus
San Diego Zoo

Other *ZOOBOOKS* titles:

Alligators & Crocodiles; Animal Babies;
Animal Champions; Animal Champions 2;
Animal Wonders; Apes; Baby Animals;
Baby Animals 2; Bats; Bears; Big Cats;
Birds of Prey; Butterflies; Camels; Cheetahs;
Chimpanzees; City Animals; The Deer Family;
Dinosaurs; Dolphins & Porpoises;
Ducks, Geese, & Swans; Eagles; Elephants;
Endangered Animals; Giraffes; Gorillas;
Hippos; Hummingbirds; Insects; Insects 2;
Kangaroos; Koalas; Lions; Little Cats;
Nocturnal Animals; Old World Monkeys;
Orangutans; Ostriches; Owls; Pandas;
Parrots; Penguins; Polar Bears; Rattlesnakes;
Rhinos; Seabirds; Seals & Sea Lions; Sea
Otters; Sharing The World With Animals;
Sharks; Skunks & Their Relatives; Snakes;
Spiders; Tigers; Turtles & Tortoises; Whales;
Wild Dogs; Wild Horses; Wolves; Zebras.

Production Manager
Laurie Nichols

Editorial Production
Marjorie Shaw
Renee C. Burch

Production Artist
Jim Webb

Circulation Manager
Demetrius Griggsby

Circulation
Shirley Patino
Maria Estrella
LaFonda Ryales

Controller
Cecil Kincaid, Jr.

Accounting & Administration
Sandra A. Battah
Paula Dennis
Jenny Sparling

Website Manager
Debra S. Barrett

Director of Sales & Marketing
Julaine Chattaway Rich

Sales
Rejina Freeman
Sally Mercer
Lori Kolb
Carmen Rodriguez

Photographic Credits
Front Cover: Michael Durham (ENP Images); **Inside Front Cover and Page One:** Jean-Paul Ferrero (Ardea London); **Page Seven: Left,** George Bryce (Animals Animals); **Middle,** Ken Fink (Ardea London); **Right,** Kenneth Fink (Ardea London); **Pages Eight and Nine:** Kenneth W. Fink (Photo Researchers); **Page Ten: Top,** G.C. Kelley (Photo Researchers); **Middle,** Academy of Natural Sciences of Philadelphia/Vireo; **Bottom,** L. Naylor (Photo Researchers); **Page Eleven: Top,** T. Parke (Vireo); **Middle,** David S. Rimlinger; **Bottom,** G. Ziesler (Peter Arnold, Inc.); **Page Twelve: Top,** Erwin & Peggy Bauer (Bruce Coleman, Inc.); **Middle,** David Madison (Bruce Coleman, Inc.); **Bottom,** Hans Reinhard (Bruce Coleman, Inc.); **Page Thirteen: Top,** Bob Campbell (Bruce Coleman, Inc.); **Middle,** Alan Weaving (Ardea London); **Bottom Left,** Jane Burton (Bruce Coleman, Inc.); **Bottom Right,** Hans Reinhard (Bruce Coleman, Inc.); **Page Fourteen: Top,** Erwin & Peggy Bauer (Bruce Coleman, Inc.); **Middle,** David Madison (Bruce Coleman, Inc.); **Bottom,** Hans Reinhard (Bruce Coleman, Inc.); **Page Fifteen: Top,** Bob Campbell (Bruce Coleman, Inc.); **Middle,** Alan Weaving (Ardea London); **Bottom Left,** Jane Burton (Bruce Coleman, Inc.); **Bottom Right,** Hans Reinhard (Bruce Coleman, Inc.); **Page Sixteen and Inside Back Cover:** IFA (Bruce Coleman, Inc.).

Art Credits
Pages Two and Three: Trevor Boyer; **Pages Four and Five:** Trevor Boyer; **Page Four: Bottom Left,** Raul Espinoza; **Pages Six and Seven:** Trevor Boyer; **Page Six: Bottom Left,** Walter Stuart; **Page Seven: Top, Center, and Bottom,** Walter Stuart; **Pages Ten and Eleven:** Trevor Boyer; **Page Ten: Bottom Left,** Walter Stuart; **Pages Twelve and Thirteen:** Barbara Hoopes; **Pages Fourteen and Fifteen:** Barbara Hoopes; **Page Fourteen: Top, Middle, and Bottom,** Walter Stuart; **Page Fifteen: Top, Middle, Bottom Left and Right,** Walter Stuart.

Printed in the U.S.A.

Wildlife Education, Ltd.
12233 Thatcher Court
Poway, California 92064-6880
www.zoobooks.com

ISBN 0-937934-27-5